Rita Mae Brown

POEMS

Rita Mae Brown

POEMS

The Crossing Press / Freedom, California 95019

The Hand That Cradles The Rock was first printed by New
York University Press.

Songs to a Handsome Woman was first printed by Diana
Press.

ISBN 0-89594-247-X, paperback
ISBN 0-89594-248-8, cloth

Another Time In The Same Place

"Tempus fugit" is what our Roman ancestors said about time, time flies. Other people say, "Time marches on," or "Time waits for no one." A more emotional soul might dredge up the old phrase, "Time is a river." In fact, I don't think that Time is any of these things. Time is an imp. This devilish imp tweaks humans because only humans have developed a sense of history and only humans have been foolish enough to write down their own personal histories.

Were I a cat, surely a more highly evolved life form than the human, I wouldn't worry about time, I wouldn't care about what I was, what I am and what I might become. I would simply exist quite gloriously in the present. Being human I do not have the natural advantages of the cat. A vague sense of time has given way to a more acute sense of its passing. The imp I rarely saw in my childhood now sits on my shoulder and whispers in my ear, "Life is short."

Upon re-reading these volumes of poetry I realized that in a funny way I was being reintroduced to myself as a young person. Amend that: a young brash person. A few of the poems I wrote in *The Hand That Cradles the Rock* I wrote at age eighteen. That was twenty four years ago. At that time I was reading about four to five hours of Latin a day. I was beginning to learn Attic Greek, a torment reserved for the damned. If you really want to make yourself miserable, crack the covers of Thucydides. My poetry reflected my literary mentors at the time, which is not to say they should bear responsibility for my stinkers.

Time had not teased me. I thought eternity was mine in which to live and in which to write. Thinking myself amazingly intelligent, I saw no reason to hide my light under a bushel basket. My youthful poetry paraded my stuff. I imitated Horace shamelessly; he still remains one of my favorite poets in the original Latin but I have grown up enough not to imitate him. Who could? There will only be one Horace.

Perhaps there will only be one Rita Mae. I'm not sure I could stand another one. Anyway, as I learned more and more about language and literature I also learned more and more about my own limitations. I wanted to write a perfect poem. I was soon humbled and wanted to write a great poem. I eventually became realistic: I wanted to write a good poem.

By the end of *The Hand That Cradles the Rock* I had produced a few poems of which I was not ashamed. I was twenty four when the poetry was published to the usual deafening silence. It remains a curiosity to me that the English language lends itself to masterful poetic expression and yet Americans display scant interest in this activity.

The two loves of my life, poetry and the theater, were going to keep me in the poverty to which I was born. This was not an appetizing prospect. Even while I continued (and still continue) to write poetry, I learned to write prose. As I was writing my first novel, *Rubyfruit Jungle,* I was also writing the second volume of poetry, *Songs to a Handsome Woman.*

Love poetry errs on the side of passion and mine certainly did. Occasionally the technique could carry the emotion, but usually the emotion spills all over the page. What is there about love that makes us so sloppy? Desipte that, the girders of Latin remained. Had I not had such a rigorous classical training, I think *Songs to a Handsome Woman* would have become an epic of ardor.

But Time, our imp, plays with me again. As a youth the poetry, despite its technical flaws, seemed okay. At the cusp of middle age I wonder how I could have ever felt that way, much less written about it. It isn't that I no longer believe in love but that my typical preoccupation with romantic love has given way to a focusing on the love that lasts, or marathon love. I suppose if it were not for romantic love laced with lust none of us would ever link up with another person. Mother used to say, "Love is what happens to people who don't know each other." It's the love that develops as we do know each other that fascinates me now. And I write poetry about it but I don't publish it. There are boxes in my library filled with poetry in varying states of undress. I haven't the time to polish the work and therefore it doesn't get published. You wouldn't send your child out naked would you? Neither will I.

I am grateful to Crossing Press for re-releasing these early works. I'm even grateful to myself for having written the poetry. I never was afraid to take chances, to tell the truth as I perceived it, no matter how unpopular. As some of the poetry grapples with being a woman loving another woman, as well as the early anti-war poetry, I was accustomed to taking my lumps. Time hasn't weakened that part of my personality at all. It's still easier to take a blow from outside than it is to be disgusted with myself for not taking a stand. I don't know how people can live and not fight back but apparently millions do. They must hate themselves.

As for loving a woman, I have never understood why some people had a fit. I still don't. It seems fine to me. If an individual is productive, responsible, and energetic, why should her choice of a partner make such a fuss? The government is only too happy to take my tax money and yet they uphold legislation that keeps me a second class citizen. Surely, there should be a tax break for those of us who are robbed of full and equal participation and protection in the life of our nation.

I have always felt that the key to a relationship is the quality of that relationship, not the sex of the people involved. Wife beating, child abuse, and mental cruelty are epidemic in our society and those horrors breed in heterosexual relationships. But a heterosexual child molestor ''on the books" has more rights, is more "normal" than I am. You figure it out. I can't.

What I can figure out is that there's no such thing as an easy life and we must each struggle for justice for ourselves and for others. Poetry is part of that struggle. The arts alert us first to where the injustices hide and, of course, they hide in each of us. There is no such thing as a perfect person, just as there is no such thing as a perfect system. But we can try, just as we can try to write perfect poetry, and then settle for good poetry and hope for the best even as we work.

If my work, this young work, makes you remember the times, remember yourself, I'm glad of it. If you're young now and it speaks to you, I am grateful. But no matter where you are in your life, I hope one or two of these poems will jolt you into thinking about yourself and the country in which we live. We have murder in abundance, greed, poverty, ignorance, and betrayal of the public by our elected officials. So do other countries. We also have a fairly fluid social set-up so people can move upwards economically with a measure of hard work and some luck. Compared with other Western nations we enjoy the freedom that is part of that Western heritage. I mention a few of our virtues to offset our faults and so that you might realize I do love my country very much. But I have never confused patriotism with blindness. We're Americans. We can do better. We have it within our power to relieve the poor, comfort the battered, and protect our minorities from those who would seek to harm them. We have the ability to be the Athens of modern times as opposed to the militaristic Sparta. I remind you that the Athenians wrote poetry. The Spartans did not.

Time will tell.

4 August 1987   Rita Mae Brown
Charlottesville, VA

The Hand That Cradles The Rock

Dedicated to women everywhere

Necropolis

These sanctified vegetables
Stunted fruits in fallow fields,
Eunuchs, caricatured human beings,
These scholars
Translating ignorance into Latin and Greek;
Tittering over beds long rotted to earth,
Endlessly dissecting the cadaver of a nun.
These secure hypocrites
Embalmed in an equinox of vanity.
Lead on! Lead on! Lead on!
How easy to be king
When all your subjects are dead.
Archaeological beings
Preserved in penultimate time.
Drone, drone
Drone your dreary dithyrambs
You stillborn, celibate intellects.
You fools, you frauds
You accumulated postules of useless learning,
Damned as mummified moles burrowing feverishly
Under Cheops immobile sands
The curse of the makers upon you.

On The Rooftop Where
All The Pigeons Go To Die

A Litany for the Male Culture

Ghosts of pigeons police their bones
And forgotten feathers bejeweled as
  white spiders spin in memory of
  starboard lights and phosphorescent tortoises;
Before great hulks of decomposed intelligence
  bobbled on the Hudson flowing endlessly
  to the wastelands of the sea,
Before dirtied seagulls with leather lungs had
  sung a dirge for the passing of pigeons
  and the senseless slaughter of insects,
Before universities and warmakers fed off each other
  like incestuous crabs;
When grasshoppers hoarded sunshine
  and sang of tulips, fat and fine,
Before a battleship passed behind my spine,
When magnificent morning glories praised the days
Before the Titanic sailed beneath the waves,
  lights ablaze,
Showing ice fish threading a sunken temple of Jupiter's
  ancient encrusted marble maze.
Now triplets of nucleotides dance in their head
They dig subways to ignore the pigeon dead.

The pigeons fly low
Wing tip to wing tip they haunt the sky
Above the businessman and my naked eye.
The wasp, unmoved, stuffs her nest with paralyzed spiders.
Frogs prophesy in the name of the Great Blue Light.
Solar winds clash with the night

Rats, afraid, run beneath the Milky Way.
Some lost dinosaur is crawling out a blistering egg
To hunt her heir unto this day.

Men fall into doubt
Clutching it in lieu of the truth.

For Joan Bird

Her name hangs heavy on my lips
In long nights I dream
A bright ringed hallucination
I reach and find her taken.

Radical Man

Witness his ego
How it flies
Up from earth
Seeing no other
In rarefied atmosphere
It congratulates itself
On its epoxied excellence,
The Eternal I,
A marvelous me of malevolence
Such is my brother
Such is our age.

The Disconnection

Strings lay all about
She told me
Strings and threads lay all about
And none of them connected
Or touched her outstretched hand.
She held out her hand to me,
It seems a year behind
She held out her hand
And I reached back with mine.
But the strings and threads tied up her brain
And she cried in anguish
She cried my name
Let go my hand to cradle her head
And now she sits alone
She sits and cradles her head
Afraid that it will roll away,
Too tired to cut it off.

For Men Only

I took him in
I can say no more
I took him in
And he lived there and
      died
A creature of time.
While I
Like the tide
Washed him in wave
After wave of eternity
That he might understand immortality
      before he goes
To the grave.
All men must die.
But I
Return to the ocean
Rolling centuries in a kiss
And lap at the moon
Until the eye of god
or locusts
Fix us
Still.

The Etruscan Queen

Inspects ancient bathrooms
See how she goes
Through Tuscan tidbits
Climbing dusty orgasms
To the touch of an archaic crotch
Long discarded underpants,
Holy vestige, pre-Roman relic
What joy. What knowledge. What truth.
"Oh and did you know
their shoes changed to pointed toe
around 550 B.C., can you see?"
She troubles herself about Etruscan clothes,
"Did their whores wear red hose?"
We costume our poor to hide their rags
She wonders were there well dresssed fags.

For Sweet Ellen

Sometime I look at you and wonder
How was it you
Were pulled under
And not myself?
Trapped in an undertow of pea-green rooms,
Fourteen months you were coming up
From the sea of the mind drowned;
Coming to the beach
Where I
The first amphibian
Was moving unused legs.

"A case of jam tomorrow and never jam today."
— Alice in Wonderland

The New Lost Feminist

A Triptych

The Center Panel:

In the twilight of the Supreme Court
Wrinkled robed children
Passed judgement on Whistling lollipops and women.
Goliath staggers, his briefcase hemorrhaging with deals.
The Court hears the last appeal
For a land where means do not devour ends.

The underground railway smuggles giant blacks and
Glistening women to hidden empires beneath the polar caps.
America's rotting rib cage frames the gallows
Of her putrid goals.
How the nation rolls to stand on its feet
An upturned crab as decayed as its prey.
The young vomit and turn away.

Underground stations fill with blacks,
Women and the young
Fleeing a Troy that has built its own horse
America becomes a bloated corpse.

The New Lost Feminist

The Right Panel:

How this beast follows us
His leprous shadow blending with our own
And we fall to fighting among ourselves
Clawing the silk cheeks of other women.

Was there a golden age to remember?
Was there a time when we knew our name
And called up great cities within us,
Our voices ringing out tidings of future nations?
Did we walk past ziggarats then as now
Heads bowed, shameful as a conquered race?
Was there ever a time?

Women, women limping on the edges of the History of Man
Crippled for centuries and dragging the heavy emptiness
Past submission and sorrow to forgotten and unknown selves.
It's time to break and run.

The New Lost Feminist

The Left Panel:

Incoherent in the midst of men
I bleed at the mouth
Gushing broken participles
And teeth cracked on bullet words.
I bleed for want of a single, precious word,
Dying in the network of swollen blue veins
Large with my life force.
How can you turn away and chatter in your small change
Of prefixes and suffixes?
A woman is dying for want of a single unrealized word,
Freedom.

"A silver crab on mica sands
Sideways she moves toward a bleeding sun."
— R.M.B.

Canto   Cantare   Cantavi   Cantatum

I sing of a woman and summer
Of hot days within my limbs
July of months and blazing woman
Who comes before me, burning, burning
Whose eyes stir sulfur seas inside
To collide with the shores of silence.
I sing of a woman and summer
The woman loves another:
I burn as a lonely taper
In blackest night

Rhadamanthos

Love knows no justice
Fruits fall from trees
An overripe tangerine
Entertains merry ants
Is as love to the hands
That never took it from the tree.

The Midnight Caesura

At the end of the afternoon
She kindly disengaged me
Or was I abandoned?
No matter what the term,
She let me go
Alone to my bed
Where her name is sewn
Along the edges of my dreams.

Fire Island

The sea is obsidian
The sea is jade
The sea is a thousand Iroquois arrowheads
Piercing the shore.
My body is borne over the sea
I move on the backs of fishes
Swimming toward an island of cannibals
Ravenous for large, juicy genitals.
My body rises and my body falls
Listing toward the open air asylum,
Where I, as a woman
Shall walk on the bones of men
Ignoring the sacramental siphoned skull
Whose capped and sterile teeth
Whisper the great lie, "Love."

Bullseye

The Epoch Begins July 20, 1969

Lions' teeth lay yellow in the grass
Along with the eye of the day
Impaled on milken spikes.
A year throbs in a rib cage.
Phantom Incas and Aztecs calculate upon great golden calendars
Trapping time between betrayed stars.
And men pretend to grow
According to the sequence of Arabic numerals
Beat out in the prisoner's rhythmic thrashing.

Dead men climb pyramids to read the sky
And pray for the female centaur
Whose great and curved bow
Lets fly the arrow
To pin the millennium like a poisonous eagle
To a rotted tree.

A thousand years is as a day
When murderers manipulate timetables
Set for planetary rape.
Woman, put your ear to your breast.
Hoofbeats.

Being

Should she leave me
I, as a bee
Stepped on and stinging
Try to fly
Spinning out my entrails
To sputter and die
Soft guts superimposed
Upon the uninterested sky.
Smashed as all images must be
And the bee
Falls back to earth
Not far from her sting
A tiny black and yellow bundle
Her transparent wings
Nervously beating life's last pulses
Wings on which life and love etched
Opposing answers
To the question outlined by the soft coil
Of her insides
Spread along the ground.

New York City

Smokestacks point at polluted skies
Amputated fingers stuck in our eyes,
Great glass altars stand in precision
Singing stacatto hymns to corporate vision.

An awesome jewel
An awesome jewel
Awaiting the Second Coming
Any second coming.

We come to Manhattan
We come bent with mortality
We come to catch sight of a flawed diamond
Aflame with imperfection
Red with blood and the sun
And still we come
Spat out like seed pods
Driven toward hard ground
We fall among the skyscrapers
To perish without light
And still we come
To see a city sanctified in emphatic communion
Millions of unwatered sinners withering together,
The human reunion.

Orphans cling to a country
As children to a father
There's no love but still it's home
As you leave in wider and wider circles
Turning to where the center should be,
Amerika.
You find him, syphilitic whore
An international festering sore.

Original Sin

This hand behind my back
Holding the other
As if some brother
Clutching its partner in crime,
The sins of the right hand.
Ten tight witnesses
Interlocking,
A hung jury
Locked in the fingers of indecision
As a hand fills a hand
In loneliness
Its other;
Awaiting, awaiting another.

The Twentyfirst Century

Let me go
From this day forward
Brighter than one thousand suns
Proclaiming love
Without a word.
There are no bottoms to words,
The bottoms have fallen out
Broken cups
Too cheap to hold, "I love you,"
The bottoms have fallen out of words
And cloak-like I cover you
Catching the honey from your lips and thighs
Where love lies.
Holding you
While language collapses around us.
I love you is on touching tongues
Silent in their meeting.
With this communion now,
Let me go
From this day forward
Brighter than one thousand suns
Lighting the way for you alone.
Lost searchers for the Holy Grail will
Follow us into the Twentyfirst Century.

To My Wife

Who is not my wife
Nor bound to me by paper
Nor am I to her
Bound as husband or wife.
I call her, Wife,
A paltry proper noun
Trying to encompass
"Until death us do part."

Silently we are cementing our lives
As a coral reef is built
Blossoming into iridescence
Providing homes for wandering Angel fish
And other bits of beauty.
Like the reefs
When we ourselves have died
The skeletons of our life work
Will still give homes to sea orphans
Swimming in waters of absurdity.

Dancing The Shout To The True Gospel
or
The Song My Movement Sisters
Won't Let Me Sing

I follow the scent of a woman
Melon heavy
Ripe with joy
Inspiring me
To rip great holes in the night
So the sun blasts through.
And this is all I shall ever know:
Her breath
Filling the hollows of my neck
A luxury diminishing death.

Hymn To The 10,000 Who Die Each Year On The Abortionist's Table In Amerika

Let us make death masks
And run our fingers over them
Searching
In the crevices of the slain faces
For slivers of truth
Which prick our fingers
Drawing blood to the sunlight
Though painful in its pushing
We must hunt as wounded women
The balm to heal one another.

The Invisible Sovereign

I have sat upon this pile of broken bottles
Feeling the pain no longer
Until I shift my weight
And am cut anew.
As blind men fear glass
I fear and find myself amid the terror,
A forest of frightening familiars.
Blind go I
But for her voice
Calling me through a smashed world
And calling up the awesome world within me.
Strangely, she stops now and then.
And you can see me, unseeing
Perched atop this decomposed glass city
Like some emaciated scarecrow
Ravaged by ulcerous holes within
Where a world once was,
Listening, listening.

The New Litany

Compounded in confusion
A mute, prosaic Sappho, I pray
"Oh let me dumb be blessed with song
To fling at the metaphors of darkness
Cemented in silence of swift time
On this side of morning;
To bring the dawn and reign Time's ravenous mouth,
To spend the sacraments on sheets
Redeemed in a kiss,
To proclaim New Christmas
The carol chanted by her eyes."
All this splendor, I pray
A groundling with face upturned
To the snow fallen down
In the night of her hair
Above me.
Deaf to my song?
Would she feign deafness
Or wave me away?
Ah, I'm left to pray,
As Venus in her ascendency
Draws triangulations on reality.

Love on The Run
or
The Trackshoe Sonata

Ask me
Do I love her?
I would have to answer,
Yes.
For I have smelled laughter
Lurking in the folds of her dress,
I have felt her hard beating and half mended heart
And sang litanies upon her breast.
Ask me,
Do I love her?
Yes, yes, yes.

Song Of My Wealth

I shall whisper in the nautilus of your ear
Songs of dolphins dying in Floridean seas
Reborn as jewel encrusted pins
Poised, surfaced in the windows of Tiffany and Sons
So far from my reach.
But let me take you to the cool sands continually cleaned
By scuttling claws of chambermaid crabs,
Where tiny birds with invisible knees stoop to pick what they missed.
Schools of night fish flash fire under the moon
Synchronized silver on a string
Pursued by a steel-blue rapier
Barracuda that knifes through jetties
Grinning in his rows of terrible sharp teeth.
A manta ray flaps his wide wings
Slow in his slender beauty
And the moon slides over the upturned tips
Spreading light over all
Clothing us in splendid silver garments
As we lay naked
Amid stars and starfish and shooting stars within us.
There open the oyster of myself
Wherein the blood pearl was a long time making
A piece of suffering enameled to joy.
Take it
This pearl
This soul which never wanders
Let others gaze in store front windows
Take it.

Song Of A Poor Young Woman

White feathered palms tremble
Beneath my spreading fingertips
I'm lined with mother-of-pearl
Silver snails with opal tails
Slide beneath my skull
My bones are gilded and slim.
Emeralds and topaz hide behind my eyes
Unblinking before all earth.
Sapphire lizards send fire along my tongue
And I burn for centuries unborn.

A Journey Into The Eyeless Sockets
Of The Night

This is the day of my majority
This is the day I,
Dying, plowed the sea
And planted dead trees,
Feeling my youth go through my fingers
Like a razor to the bone.
I have come to the threshold of pain
An unwilling bride
Carried by pride
Across jaws of broken promises
To bear in this depth, sorrow.
Should I die in childbirth
They will call it suicide
As I cry for one finger of the dawn.

The Female Of The Species

Like the lioness wounded, disconsolate
I roar and bend the grasses
Driving tender antelopes
Through hushed savannahs
So none may scent the side's deepening wound
Lions listen in the pride, cowed
As the lioness lopes a hardened silhouette
Across the cruel and lovely plain
To die on the run.

The Middle Class Identity Crisis Viewed Through The Eyes Of Poor White Trash

I am not the same
I am not the same,
Where is the name behind my name?
The laugh behind my lips?
My face's secret is reflected
Bouncing back from broken mirrors
Fragments of an inoffensive caricature
Fused into a patchwork quilt of being.

The anguish of fall
Sent inarticulate sorrow
Far within the bone.
A ship's horn on the Hudson
Announced winter's advent
Leaves bend their knees
Out of respect
For the dying grass
And I walk home alone.

Aristophanes' Symposium

I have known it from the beginning
As though by fate
Disbelieving fate.
That we as one
Were divided by some awful hand
And I have searched the centuries for your face,
Hearing eons echo your name,
A muffled refrain drenched in longing.
Long have I yearned,
Spurning women
All women save the one I knew
In thick clouds of prehistory.
Even Helen was a bone
I threw to Paris
Outraged at her imperfection.
I toiled, a plaything of Cronos
From Genesis through silly flocks of years
Herding decades into the penumbra of my brain
Poking shadows of bleating days for your face.
The years slipped by
And I alone felt them go
No longer counting sheep
Too tired for counting sheep
But I will know you as you know me
And one day you will call me, "Woman."

A Song For Winds And My Vassar Women

Here among the trees
The world takes the shape of a woman's body
And there is beauty in the place
Lips touch
But minds miss the vital connection
And hearts wander
Down dormitory halls
More hurt than hollow.

The Self Affirms Herself

Neither stars nor gods can guide me
A law unto myself
And a self apart
I move in the shadow of the great guillotine
That rhythmically does its work
On heads remaining unbowed.

The Bourgeois Questions

"I wonder about the burn
Behind your eyes,
What is it in you that disquiets me so?
Do you hate me for my softness?"

"No, I've come through a land
You'll never know."

The Arrogance Of Immortality

The difference between
My little cat
And I
Is
That I
Know
I am going to die.

Cygne

Sings the swan
Her song of aching beauty
Neck outstretched to question the sky
Then coils and pierces her breast
That houses the song.
So sing I,
"Amerika, Amerika."

Horse Sense

Summer smolders
And days draw long
Grapevines roll to the sea,
I ride through a field of Queen Anne's lace,
Heather and blue pine,
Come kind horse and lead the way
To beach plums, life and immortal play.

For Lydia French
(Shot and killed, August 13, 1970)

Women know
Women have always known
As marrow to the bone
Death is at the heart of men.

I touch your solitary, senseless death
And run for my life.
Men shall yet know
The fruits earned
Of death.
Goodbye, Lydia

The President's Bedchamber

He lies awake at night
With his hand over his heart
Because he is not sure
If it's still there.

The Great Pussblossom

Hoisting her tail to the vertical
Pussblossom plants a kiss of suspicion upon her spouse,
"Tell me, dear, have you been eating mouse?"

Clytemnestra's Song

He yielded to me
And I felt his body
Go under mine
Like an enemy last conquered.
What ecstasy, a just death!

A Short Note For Liberals

I've seen your kind before
Forty plus and secure
Settling for a kiss from feeble winds
And calling it a storm.

Macho

The lamplites are lit with blood
How can we find our way home
Where mother washes our agony and
Hangs it on the line to dry?
In these times is it proper for men to cry?

The Marriage Hearse

Tell me the story of your love
And how it died
Like worn winds torn on
Winter's jagged branches.
How you, found the lie
Deep within the kiss.

History Reappears In The Dead Of Night

I dreamed I spoke in foreign tongues
Thick liqueurs
Dark as the dawn,
Oh, Byzantium.

Sunset

I ride in Central Park
To see the buildings rise
Like dusty rose madonnas
Lifting huge shoulders to the sky
I ride and say farewell
To a doomed city to die.

The Women's House Of Detention

Here amid the nightsticks, handcuffs and interrogation
Inside the cells, beatings, the degradation
We grew a strong and bitter root
That promises justice.

Song Of The Subway

There is a longing in the subway
Rising from the damp sour tracks
Seizing our nostrils until they ache.
Beauty, the people want beauty.

Past our longing speeds the empty train
Headlights smashed and whistle shrill
A ghost train shuttling to a caterpillar's grave.
The people watch, silent and still.

Overhead, business men carry laundry bags
Filled with dirty dreams.
Will the train never come?
Beauty, the people want . . . .

Promittor

Dew falls on the oysters at low tide
And the sea is ablaze with pearls.
I ride a horse to moongate
Where the water's fire
Lights the backbones of prehistoric fish
Tangled in my brain.

The Nihilist

I know nothing
Neither life nor death
Yet I live
Brutalized, stupid, dumb
I live to cling
To climb
To cry, "I am."

For Madam Binh

The birds bow before me
And dogs mourne my step
Such is my anguish
Such, my despair.
The pure who plunder not
Are butchered, stripped and left to rot.

Elle

Someone wrote in French
"Where are the snows of yesteryear?"
And I reply in English
"In my heart, in my heart."

The Awakening

Men's arteries are turning to stone.
The owl of Athena takes wing
Only at dusk
And brushes the eyelids of Amazons
Who soldier their shields
And promise fresh blood
To make the trees grow
From dead sparrows' throats.

St. Zita's Home For Friendless Women

The unwed
Eyes downcast
Pass each other like
Dumb cargo ships
Sailing over dirty tile floors
Eyeless as their unborn
They ignore each other
And steam to watery graves.

Sappho's Reply

My voice rings down through thousands of years
To coil around your body and give you strength,
You who have wept in direct sunlight,
Who have hungered in invisible chains,
Tremble to the cadence of my legacy:
An army of lovers shall not fail.

Feminist

Having slumbered
She rose and shook
Victorian shadows from her hair.

Songs To A Handsome Woman

To The Handsome Woman:

Slip this book inside your blouse
To lie against your heart
In innocence.

To the Reader:

This is a book of love poems, poems inspired by a single individual. Against my will, my "rational" self, I fell in love. I can't logically explain it. I could say I was drawn to a fine artist and nurtured my own art from her brilliance . . . or the flesh was impaled on beauty . . . or the mind rejoiced in her wit. But that explains nothing. No one will ever explain love and while I may be fool enough to be open about my feelings, I'm not fool enough to try to explain the unexplainable.

But I can say this about love . . . it deepens experience, making all life exquisite and valuable. The destruction of individuals, races, classes, sexes, is doubly repulsive when you have brushed against joy. The miracle of love, for me, at least, is that it recommits me to struggle on new levels. You see, it's a very simple connection to understand that a society or individual who denies love is a step away from denying life.

Kisses and Revolution,

Rita Mae Brown

Follies

This is a poem to knock at your doors
A simple verse and pure
       a medieval tapestry
Free from judicious hints and careful indiscretions
Bright as the stage lights
       hot upon your handsome face
This is a poem to praise your days
You, who have
Crossed the line between craft and creation.

The Midnight Follies Or Mary's Ass

In the science of the night
In the recollected light
In that hour when intellect reaches its zenith
Unleash the dark horses
To ride against the pulse of reason,
The anarchy of instinct,
Primitive treason
That hangs on the short end of a promise,
Love
Ageless epiphany
Leading me to follow a movie star.
Bethlehem,
How you've changed!
(I think I'll make the journey by car.)

Travelogue

I took the woman's face
To be the roadmap of her self,
And rode past temples of beauty
       through schools of thought
To a soft meadow of kindness
And I would have laid my body there
But from my own green kindness
Instead, I laid my soul.

The Sun In January

She broke down the four walls of my mind
And left behind
A sweet, clean and endless prairie.

Dedicated To All Women Who Haven't Loved A Woman

Must you run from me?
Are my hands so different from a man's?
Or my lips too full and soft?
Do my eyes affect you oddly?
Is my body so strange in its familiarity?
Am I so different?
Is my love so terrible?
Or is the fear growing from some deeper root
Understood only by poets and weeping mothers?
Must you run from windows beneath the skin?
Listen, your answer may be different than mine
But don't run from the question.

To My Dream Butch Straight Lady Who Bolts Her Doors But Leaves Her Windows Unlatched

I will not sneak through narrow trails
  of permanent subversion
You are the one I love.
It's not my fault we're both women
Why hold it against me?

For The Japanese Silk
In Her Ladysmith's Mind

My heart's not broken—
Just ruptured.

A Woman Wronged

She's a lonesome woman
For I've seen her weep
There in harbor mists
A useless token
She keeps a desecrated flame
Yet holds it high
For in her iron crowned head
There lingers metallic a hollow ring
Which only the young can hear—
Thousands of ragged, shuffling feet:
"Give me your poor, your tired, your huddled masses
Longing to be free."

December 17, 1971 To December 17, 1972
A Narrative, Of Sorts

She wore a red dress
The first time I saw her
She just appeared in that awful red dress
Out of nowhere
On December 17, 1971.
Later in January, I met her.
A strange turn at the edge of her mouth
Gave her away.
Once she took me to dinner,
You're surprised?
Well, I'm amusing sometimes.
Like an honest fool
I asked her to go to bed with me.
She drifted off after that
But I knew she was out there,
Like a ship in the fog
I could feel her magnificent dimensions.

You've asked me about her so many times
That's why I'm telling you all this.
I don't like to talk about her, you see
She hurts me in some hidden place.
And yes, she does party with cold warriors
        and aging debutantes.
She's innocent in her ignorance
Drinking Mexican beer on the other side
        of the barricades.
I tell you she doesn't understand.
She thinks in terms of people
Not politics.

She thinks she's paid for acting
She doesn't know she lives off the poor.
She does know there's a movement,
She's read about it in the papers
But she doesn't understand that there's
     going to be a Revolution,
And she wouldn't believe in it anyway.
After all, her friends went to Eastern Europe
And those people over there aren't free.
She doesn't understand
She's on the wrong side by default
Believing she's not on either side
Because she's not a joiner.
I tell you she is not the enemy.
She's only a woman who wants to be left alone
To do as she pleases
And it doesn't please her
To ask the kind of questions we're asking.
And who can blame her?
For the truth is told with hate
And lies are told with love.

Language is the roadmap of a culture
And this is when the language leaves me
As wind before water
This is no longer a poem
This is an effort
To find a form for the unspeakable.
Wake up, sisters!
Wake up, my beautiful, my handsome woman

Our country is lost
Our citizens are dying
The world is unravelling
And the sun hides the stars in a lie of light.
There are those who walk this earth
Who would destroy us all.
Wake up, people
To this, the cruelest thought:
As the beast stalks the land
So the beast lies within
Each of us
Even her breast
Even mine
And these tears making a mockery of my courage
Are for my pain
Are for the beast within us and the saint as well
And for her
Because a butterfly is folding its wings.

Darkness, Dreams And Death

I've seen my death mirrored in the darkness of my dreams
Like a tongue returning to the site of the missing tooth
I come back
Crying, "No."

I've seen my dreams mirrored in the darkness of my death
Like a fly lusting for the final, perfect spiderweb
I go out
Laughing, "Death's an easy lie."

I've seen my darkness mirrored in the death of my dreams.
Like a prophet running down shadows of words to meaning
I tell you
"Fight in the endless war of truth against truth."

A Pink Chambered Nautilus

A pink chambered nautilus
Her womb whispers songs of the sea
Oh, yes
Say yes
And come make love with me.

Who was born on the same day as the Handsome Woman and who died on the day I met her. Life is so full of twists and turns. This is one of them and I shall never comprehend it.

Death In Absentia
For Carole Slader

In the structure of her veins
        I found the pulse of her fortune.
She's found the secret of the moths
        traced in wet earthworm trails.
Yes, the weakness of the living
        is in attaching importance
        to the bones of the dead
But, oh, the line between life and death
        is not where we thought it was.
Dead, my love?
Like a pebble in my shoe
I'll walk with you for the remainder of my days.
Dead, my love.

The Ides Of Age

Her eyes
Pressed a thorn into my chest
A red rose slowly bled white
My youth drips from me
In this silence
For she will not speak.
Youth would find it easy to die
But my new age tells me,
"Wait."
No woman born can be so cruel.

On Being An Orphan At Age 27

Please
Let me put my arms around your neck
And lean on you for awhile.
My sisters have betrayed me
And my brothers are blind.
The wind is an icy knife
When stars have fled the night
And I've no gods to call on
Save a woman's heart.
So let me put my arms around your neck
And hold me for awhile.

For Those Of Us Working For A New World

The dead are the only people
    to have permanent dwellings.
We, nomads of Revolution
Wander over the desolation of many generations
And are reborn on each other's lips
To ride wild mares over unfathomable canyons
Heralding dawns, dreams and sweet desire.

True Confessions

In the face of her beauty
My rhythm shudders
And I am no longer a poet
But just another woman in love.

Spontaneous Combustion

Will my heredity
    catch up with me
Like some sinister puzzle
    pieced together with age?
Is there a heredity to catch me?
Or do my corpuscles
Function
Ignorant of Mother and Father
As my brain?

Beyond Vocabulary

Her hands, strong
Carry gold rings
One flourish, one gesture
She tells you things.
Palm upturned
She pleads her case,
Fingers extended
She defines her space.
Her craft demands
She have fine hands.

The Last Politic

On my bed in the silence of the moon
I know we are all imprisoned by our rib cage
In the end betrayed by our own bodies.

Poetic Ellipsis

She came at that precise junction in a life
When the past is unbearable
And the future uncertain.

I Looked For Sisters Where Only Strangers Lived
A Movement Lament

These days
I feel as though I'm dying
Or is it something inside
Struggling to live?
I fear the shadows of self-hating women
Who tear for my heart
Like ego starved harpies.
I fear I shall never speak with you again.
And if you keep from me
Then let them eat my heart.
The sad blood of it
Will fill their emptiness.

The World Turns On An Unresolved Axle

Lovemaking is full of unspoken promises
Which everybody knows
But no one understands.

A Poet's Gift

Lyrics flow from my body
Onto this page of paper.
Did Shakespeare's dark lady
Lie so heavy on the page
As my heart presses here?
Did she/he run from words
That shattered safe worlds
As my lady runs from me?
The answer's been lost
In the corner of a tomb.
The dead can't help me
And the living refuse.
But the power of her promise
Overshadows even those lesbian fears
For some secret waters from which all Art flows
Runs through her and me
And tells me past Reason's rigid laws
That this thing must be.
So like my Elizabethan brother
Feverishly, I write these lines
Knowing when her curtains fall
When the costumes rot
When last she speaks her lines
These lines remain
That when we two are lost
Beneath grass and dew
These words carry what we were
And make us new.

Deja Vu
Watching Old Movies On The Late Show

Once I saw you
When you were 27.
Strange to see you
At the point I find myself.
Film makes time and history optional,
Perhaps I'm 51
and you're 27?
No,
I am 27
And you are 51.
What does it matter, anyway?
You look much the same
Handsomer now—
Except
The years are rivers
Widening our conceits into slavery
Narrowing our arteries into cowardice.
Does age really bring with it knowledge
Or is it the knowledge of self-defeat?
Did you ever have a dream above applause?
Did you strike a hard bargain with the devil of fame?
And did you lose something along the way?
You did, I know you did.
Whisper then to me
Whisper the dream quickly
Lest I become older in this instant
Intoning a catechism of congratulation
For my mind that respects no boundaries.
Whisper it
So that I might grow rather than age.

Broadway Delicatessan Lyrics
For My Musical Lady To Sing In Her Shower

Does the music of the stars disturb you?
Drink a reincarnation cocktail
And discover
We're just another pair of identical strangers
Caught between fireflies and lightning
When you were too young to know
And I know I was too young.
But now we're old enough
To be caught between bed and bedlam.
A final shrug, your oratorio of regret?
And yet, return
Trace my profile with your finger
For I am an apprentice to the future.
Touch me
And find some remnant of your forgotten self.
After all,
We're just another pair of identical strangers.

Mercy, Fairest Daughter Of Thought And Experience

Night, night
I grow sick of the night
For the flesh dreams
    of flesh and dawns
Wrapped in lover's arms
Fresh with first nakedness.
Curse this night
That breeds such dreams
Torment
To awake
And find my empty bed.
Oh, woman
If mercy is not a myth
Come find me and these dreams.

On Stage She Makes Thought Visible

Teach me what you know.
Your lips
Kissed or unkissed
Still carry on them
My salvation.

The Autograph Of A Thought

This is the last poem
I'll ever write for you.
It's been a century in my soul
Since I've heard or seen you in the flesh.
Apologies,
I know I'm free with abstract nouns
But then I haven't seen you in a muffled eon
So I've built empires with words
And cities of sounds
To ease this injurious silence.
For what?
So this can become a volume of forgotten love?
And I, without the solace of dissipation,
Am doomed to face myself in shattering mirrors.

Love, I reached and caught
My hand in the cobwebs of civilization,
Irritated, I broke a strand of that spider web.
It wept clear, silken blood
Running down my fingers to encircle my wrist.
Is this the bloodknot I am to wear
Signifying maturity?
Is this the bracelet of ceremonial conflict
Honoring the old tyrannies that return with romance?
Now, dazzling, I wear the jewels of deep wounds.

My love, you are the actress
But I, the strolling player
Am young and shining as I too
Cross the line between craft and creation
Knowing that the risk of going on stage

Is that I may be driven off.
Fearless, I am blazing into my summer
Begging you for the balance of autumnal passion
For we both know
Darwin's law applies to survival
Not success.

Yes, this is the last poem
I'll ever write for you,
Until the next one.